The Snowman

Written by Cynthia Rider,
based on the original characters
created by Roderick Hunt and Alex Brychta
Illustrated by Alex Brychta

OXFORD
UNIVERSITY PRESS

Biff   Chip   Wilma

Wilf   Kipper   Floppy

6

Wilma made a snowman.

8

It had a red nose.

It had a blue scarf.

It had green gloves.

It had a black hat.

The hat fell on Floppy.

Floppy ran.

Oh no!

No snowman!

Talk about the story

What are the colours the snowman is wearing?

Why did Floppy run off?

What else could you put on the snowman?

What would you like to make with snow or sand?

Fun activity

Find the twin snowmen.